Preface

The Declaration of Independence is one of the most profound historical documents to ever have been created. The Declaration of independence was signed on July 4th, 1776 declaring United States sovereignty and freedom.

The Declaration of Independence tells a story of tyranny and of an abuse of power by the Great Britain Royalty, during those days. This document is arguably one of the most important documents in American history.

We have added many Public Domain images to this revised edition of The Declaration of Independence, to help create the atmosphere of those days. We have also made this version to have Extra Large Font for your reading comfort. Thank you for reading and enjoy!

The United States Declaration of Independence was created by the U.S. Government on July 4th, 1776 and is considered "common property", which is also in the Public Domain.

The Inauguration of George Washington (1789)
by James H. Cafferty 1819-1869 *Public Domain*

1776

The American Declaration of Independence

Extra Large Font

Publicus Domanium

LuLu Press, Inc.
Morrisville, North Carolina

ISBN: 978-1-7948-2941-1

Cover design by James Peale 1749-1831 "George Washington (Ca. 1782)" Public Domain

Page border design by Jules Edmond Charles Lachaise (ca. 1897) "Design for a ceiling painted in filagree designs (19th Century)" Public Domain

Book design by Publicus Domanium

Printed by LuLu Press, Inc., in the United States of America

First Printing, 2021.

LuLu Press, Inc.
627 Davis Drive, Suite 300
Morrisville, North Carolina, 27560

In Congress July 4, 1776

The unanimous Declaration of the thirteen united States of America,

When in the Course of human events, it becomes necessary for one people to dissolve the political bands which have connected them with another, and to assume among the powers of the earth, the separate and equal station to which the Laws of Nature and of Nature's God entitle them, a decent respect to the opinions of mankind requires that they should declare the causes which impel them to the separation.

**Washington And Von Steuben At Valley Forge
(Ca. 1890-1896)
by Howard Pyle 1853-1911** *Public Domain*

We hold these truths to be self-evident, that all men are created equal, that they are endowed by their Creator with certain unalienable Rights, that among these are Life, Liberty and the pursuit of Happiness.

–That to secure these rights, Governments are instituted among Men, deriving their just powers from the consent of the governed,

–That whenever any Form of Government becomes destructive of these ends, it is the Right of the People to alter or to abolish it, and to institute new Government, laying its foundation on such principles

Washington and Lafayette at Mount Vernon, 1784
(The Home of Washington after the War) (1859)
by Thomas Prichard Rossiter 1818-1871 *Public Domain*

and organizing its powers in such form, as to them shall seem most likely to effect their Safety and Happiness.

Prudence, indeed, will dictate that Governments long established should not be changed for light and transient causes; and accordingly all experience hath shewn, that mankind are more disposed to suffer, while evils are sufferable, than to right themselves by abolishing the forms to which they are accustomed.

But when a long train of abuses and usurpations, pursuing invariably the same Object evinces a design to

Washington's Retreat From Great Meadows
(Ca. 1890-1896)
by Howard Pyle 1853-1896 *Public Domain*

reduce them under absolute Despotism, it is their right, it is their duty, to throw off such Government, and to provide new Guards for their future security.

–Such has been the patient sufferance of these Colonies; and such is now the necessity which constrains them to alter their former Systems of Government. The history of the present King of Great Britain is a history of repeated injuries and usurpations, all having in direct object the establishment of an absolute Tyranny over these States. To prove this, let Facts be submitted to a candid world.

The American War of Independence (Ca. 1879)
by Ludwig Rubelli von Sturmfest 1841-1905 *Public Domain*

He has refused his Assent to Laws, the most wholesome and necessary for the public good.

He has forbidden his Governors to pass Laws of immediate and pressing importance, unless suspended in their operation till his Assent should be obtained; and when so suspended, he has utterly neglected to attend to them.

He has refused to pass other Laws for the accommodation of large districts of people, unless those people would relinquish the right of Representation in the Legislature, a right

Thompson, The Clerk Of Congress, Announcing To Washington, At Mount Vernon, His Election to Presidency (Ca. 1890-1896)
by Howard Pyle 1853-1896 *Public Domain*

inestimable to them and formidable to tyrants only.

He has called together legislative bodies at places unusual, uncomfortable, and distant from the depository of their public Records, for the sole purpose of fatiguing them into compliance with his measures.

He has dissolved Representative Houses repeatedly, for opposing with manly firmness his invasions on the rights of the people.

He has refused for a long time, after such dissolutions, to cause others to be elected; whereby the Legislative powers, incapable of

Washington Crossing the Delaware (1851)
by Emanuel Gottlieb Leutze 1816-1868 *Public Domain*

annihilation, have returned to the People at large for their exercise; the State remaining in the mean time exposed to all the dangers of invasion from without, and convulsions within.

He has endeavoured to prevent the population of these States; for that purpose obstructing the Laws for Naturalization of Foreigners; refusing to pass others to encourage their migrations hither, and raising the conditions of new Appropriations of Lands.

He has obstructed the Administration of Justice, by refusing his Assent to Laws

Washington Street, Indianapolis at Dusk (1892-1895)
by Theodore Clement Steele (1847-1926) *Public Domain*

for establishing Judiciary powers.

He has made Judges dependent on his Will alone, for the tenure of their offices, and the amount and payment of their salaries.

He has erected a multitude of New Offices, and sent hither swarms of Officers to harrass our people, and eat out their substance.

He has kept among us, in times of peace, Standing Armies without the Consent of our legislatures.

He has affected to render the Military independent of and

Washington Sea Eagle (Ca. 1836-1839) by John James Audubon (1785-1851) *Public Domain*

superior to the Civil power.

He has combined with others to subject us to a jurisdiction foreign to our constitution, and unacknowledged by our laws; giving his Assent to their Acts of pretended Legislation:

For Quartering large bodies of armed troops among us:

For protecting them, by a mock Trial, from punishment for any Murders which they should commit on the Inhabitants of these States:

For cutting off our Trade with all parts of the world:

Seventh Regiment on Review, Washington Square, New York (1851)
by Otto Boetticher 1811-1886 *Public Domain*

For imposing Taxes on us without our Consent:

For depriving us in many cases, of the benefits of Trial by Jury:

For transporting us beyond Seas to be tried for pretended offences:

For abolishing the free System of English Laws in a neighbouring Province, establishing therein an Arbitrary government, and enlarging its Boundaries so as to render it at once an example and fit instrument for introducing the same absolute rule into these Colonies:

The Resignation of General Washington,
December 23, 1783 (Ca. 1824-1828)
by John Trumbull 1756-1843 *Public Domain*

For taking away our Charters, abolishing our most valuable Laws, and altering fundamentally the Forms of our Governments:

For suspending our own Legislatures, and declaring themselves invested with power to legislate for us in all cases whatsoever.

He has abdicated Government here, by declaring us out of his Protection and waging War against us.

He has plundered our seas, ravaged our Coasts, burnt our towns, and destroyed the lives of our people.

Visit of the Prince of Wales, President Buchanan, and Dignitaries to the Tomb of Washington at Mount Vernon, October 1860 (1861)
by Thomas Prichard Rossiter 1818-1871 *Public Domain*

He is at this time transporting large Armies of foreign Mercenaries to compleat the works of death, desolation and tyranny, already begun with circumstances of Cruelty & perfidy scarcely paralleled in the most barbarous ages, and totally unworthy the Head of a civilized nation.

He has constrained our fellow Citizens taken Captive on the high Seas to bear Arms against their Country, to become the executioners of their friends and Brethren, or to fall themselves by their Hands.

He has excited domestic insurrections amongst us, and

Washington's Birthday (1878)
by Charles Baugniet (1814-1886) *Public Domain*

has endeavoured to bring on the inhabitants of our frontiers, the merciless Indian Savages, whose known rule of warfare, is an undistinguished destruction of all ages, sexes and conditions.

In every stage of these Oppressions We have Petitioned for Redress in the most humble terms: Our repeated Petitions have been answered only by repeated injury. A Prince whose character is thus marked by every act which may define a Tyrant, is unfit to be the ruler of a free people.

Nor have We been wanting in attentions to our Brittish

brethren. We have warned them from time to time of attempts by their legislature to extend an unwarrantable jurisdiction over us.

We have reminded them of the circumstances of our emigration and settlement here.

We have appealed to their native justice and magnanimity, and we have conjured them by the ties of our common kindred to disavow these usurpations, which, would inevitably interrupt our connections and correspondence.

They too have been deaf to the voice of justice and of consanguinity. We must, therefore, acquiesce in the necessity, which denounces our Separation, and hold them, as we hold the rest of mankind, Enemies in War, in Peace Friends.

We, therefore, the Representatives of the united States of America, in General Congress, Assembled, appealing to the Supreme Judge of the world for the rectitude of our intentions, do, in the Name, and by Authority of the good People of these Colonies, solemnly publish and declare, That these United Colonies are, and of Right ought to be Free and Independent States;

that they are Absolved from all Allegiance to the British Crown, and that all political connection between them and the State of Great Britain, is and ought to be totally dissolved; and that as Free and Independent States, they have full Power to levy War, conclude Peace, contract Alliances, establish Commerce, and to do all other Acts and Things which Independent States may of right do.

And for the support of this Declaration, with a firm reliance on the protection of divine Providence, we mutually pledge to each other our Lives, our Fortunes and our sacred Honor.

JOHN HANCOCK, President

Attested, CHARLES THOMSON, Secretary

New Hampshire
JOSIAH BARTLETT
WILLIAM WHIPPLE
MATTHEW THORNTON

Massachusetts-Bay
SAMUEL ADAMS
JOHN ADAMS
ROBERT TREAT PAINE
ELBRIDGE GERRY

Rhode Island
STEPHEN HOPKINS
WILLIAM ELLERY

Connecticut
ROGER SHERMAN
SAMUEL HUNTINGTON
WILLIAM WILLIAMS
OLIVER WOLCOTT

Georgia
BUTTON GWINNETT
LYMAN HALL
GEO. WALTON

Maryland
SAMUEL CHASE
WILLIAM PACA
THOMAS STONE
CHARLES CARROLL OF
CARROLLTON

Virginia
GEORGE WYTHE
RICHARD HENRY LEE
THOMAS JEFFERSON
BENJAMIN HARRISON
THOMAS NELSON, JR.
FRANCIS LIGHTFOOT LEE
CARTER BRAXTON.

New York
WILLIAM FLOYD
PHILIP LIVINGSTON
FRANCIS LEWIS
LEWIS MORRIS

Pennsylvania
ROBERT MORRIS
BENJAMIN RUSH
BENJAMIN FRANKLIN
JOHN MORTON
GEORGE CLYMER
JAMES SMITH
GEORGE TAYLOR
JAMES WILSON
GEORGE ROSS

Delaware
CAESAR RODNEY
GEORGE READ
THOMAS M'KEAN

North Carolina
WILLIAM HOOPER
JOSEPH HEWES
JOHN PENN

South Carolina
EDWARD RUTLEDGE
THOMAS HEYWARD, JR.
THOMAS LYNCH, JR.
ARTHUR MIDDLETON

New Jersey
RICHARD STOCKTON
JOHN WITHERSPOON
FRANCIS HOPKINS
JOHN HART
ABRAHAM CLARK

www.ingramcontent.com/pod-product-compliance
Lightning Source LLC
Chambersburg PA
CBHW061326250726
48657CB00003B/1067